Moving on with confidence

Perceptions of success in teaching and learning adult literacy

Jan Eldred

niace

promoting adult learning

Research Paper

Contents

Introduction

This paper presents a study of the changing perceptions of success in teaching and learning adult literacy in England, and highlights emerging issues and research questions. It outlines the research methods adopted to investigate what teachers and learners, in a general further education college, thought represented success in adult literacy. The study demonstrated a range of indicators of successful teaching and learning with an almost complete agreement that success is indicated by an increase in confidence. This was identified whether learners had made tiny or massive gains in externally-measurable increases in literacy skills. The growth in confidence related to changed behaviours associated with the application of literacy in daily life and was identified by learners, tutors, families, friends and colleagues. The study examined the nature of confidence in learning, providing insight into what seems to support its development, especially in relation to adult literacy education.

The study concluded that growth in confidence is highly significant for those who teach and those who learn in adult literacy education. The changed behaviours, which form the evidence of a growth in confidence, should, therefore, be part of the process of assessing and recording success in the literacy-learning journey.

The history of adult literacy education – shifting understandings of success

For many people, adult literacy education in England and Wales began in 1974 with the Adult Literacy Campaign, known in its most public manifestation as the television programme, "On the Move". At the same time the Adult Literacy Resource Agency (ALRA) was developed with a grant of £1million to establish projects and publish resources. The majority of tutors who were trained to respond to the people coming forward for tuition were volunteers. They taught in local community centres, schools and homes. The curriculum was negotiated with the learner and related to their 'need to know' as well as interests and hobbies. Learners determined the focus of all activities and there were few or no appropriate diagnostic or assessment materials, recording or review systems. Success was determined by whether progress was being made. This was identified through reviewing completed work, assessing work which had been taught, talking about how the learner felt and her/his on-going attendance. There were no standards against which to assess progress and no accreditation or qualifications framework for the skills, knowledge and understanding developed.

By the end of the 1970s literacy had broadened to include numeracy and the term "basic education" evolved (Adult Literacy Unit, 1978). At the same time, unemployment in the industrialised world escalated and the Manpower Services Commission (MSC) began funding preparatory courses in basic skills. A divide began to emerge between the

"...*liberal curriculum, a philosophy of informal, student-centred teaching and assessment...*" (Hamilton, 1996, p154)

and the skills for employment delivered in such programmes as Training Opportunities Programmes (TOPs) and Youth Training Schemes (YTS). During the 1980s a number of Government-sponsored programmes focused on unemployed people and appeared to adopt a philosophy which suggested that they were responsible for their unemployment and therefore should gain the skills needed for a new economy. Most programmes included basic skills tuition (Avis, 1996) and success was measured in employment outcomes. A different attitude seemed to permeate the student-centred approach, which tried to remove the blame from the individual to external factors and emphasise new opportunities for learning in a different environment using methods unlike their previous experiences (Charnley and Withnall, 1989).

During the 1980s ESOL provision was added to the brief of the newly-formed Adult Literacy and Basic Skills Unit (ALBSU). The need to consider different approaches to providing basic skills tuition for them, geared to their particular interests and requirements, was identified. ALBSU indicated that the wide range of skills and abilities in speaking, listening, reading and writing English was dependent upon previous education opportunities (ALBSU, 1993).

Accreditation for work in basic skills was developed for both staff and learners at this time. Volunteer tutors were a feature of the adult literacy campaign and continue to be an important part of the provision (DfEE, 2001). Training for them and paid tutors was accredited by City and Guilds, as was the introduction of Wordpower and Numberpower as accreditation routes for learners. The links to National Vocational Qualifications (NVQs) were evident in these developments and whilst this could be welcomed for staff, questions were raised about the vocationalisation of the curriculum for learners. The focus on learning basic skills for employment and economic purposes appeared to be endorsed. Similarly the later Moser report of 1999 seemed to emphasise the economic drivers for basic skills education in the light of global competitiveness and national productivity (Moser, 1999). These emphases appeared to ignore the concept that literacy, language and numeracy are about social practices, exchanges between people, cultural activities and sense-making (Hourigan, 1994; Fingeret and Drennon, 1997; Barton, Hamilton and Ivanič, 2000). Many tutors preferred to use the accreditation routes offered by the Open College Network (OCN). These provided a wide range of unitised opportunities and the possibility of negotiating and creating accredited programmes based on learners' interests and requirements.

Until the introduction of the Further and Higher Education Act 1992, most provision of basic skills tuition had been made through Local Education Authorities (LEAs). This was usually due to the commitment of elected members and LEA officers and to the passions of tutors and managers in the FE institutions, rather than a systematic commitment to this area of work through a national policy framework. The Act enabled further education colleges to attract funding for basic skills activities in the same way as other curriculum areas. The mainstream status was welcomed (ALBSU, 1994) and its previous marginalisation acknowledged (Moser, 1999). However, this also led to a further focus on qualifications or accredited learning routes in the implementation of the funding methodology and the requirements of Management Information Systems (MIS), in order to optimise funding for institutions.

The International Adult Literacy Survey (IALS), published in 1998, provided profiles on literacy, language and numeracy in Britain and compared them with other nations, indicating the necessity for countries to be skilled for competition in a global economy. The data informed the Moser Report (1999) which recommended the introduction of new standards and a new basic skills curriculum as well as national tests. The drive for improved quality of provision was characterised by the introduction of a revised Quality Mark (BSA, 1998), a staff development programme known as the Basic Skills Quality Initiative (2000), and a strategy announced by the new Adult Basic Skills Strategy Unit (DfEE 2001). Goals were set which included "…helping 750,000 people improve basic skills by 2004" (Social Exclusion Unit, 2001, p27). These have now been revised to 1.5 million people by the year 2007. The Qualifications and Curriculum Authority (QCA) published standards for adult literacy (QCA, 2000) and the core curriculum was published in 2001 (BSA, 2001).

Whilst the movement of literacy education from the campaign of the 1970s to centre stage in 2000 was to be welcomed, a number of tensions arose for providers, practitioners and learners of basic skills.

There are suggestions that if we deal with spelling, punctuation and grammar, then literacy and language will be improved. These specific skills have been described as "…surface features…" (Hourigan, 1994, p20) and seem divorced from the complexities of literacy and language inextricably woven into home, cultural and work activities. There seem to be tensions between the Government's policies which acknowledge the wider benefits of learning to the individual, a civilised society and spiritual fulfilment (DfEE, 1998), on the one hand, and concerns to grow the economy, on the other. There is a danger, as in the 1980s, that individuals are blamed for their disadvantage and are given responsibility for tackling it (Thompson, 2001). It can be argued that developing literacy can empower people to become involved and engaged in a range of activities which question systems and inequalities and challenge injustices. Is this what is behind Government thinking, or is it a belief that improving 'technical' language and literacy skills will improve the economy and push the UK up the international competitiveness league tables?

Emerging issues

During this period of the growth of the basic skills agenda, practitioners questioned many of the policies and practices with which they were confronted. How could funding be found for outreach time and activities to reach and engage with people for whom adult learning was perceived as an irrelevance? How could staff time be found to develop their skills as well as train and support volunteers? Existing learners indicated their interest in creative and practical activities and outdoor pursuits, but how was time to be found to develop imaginative curricula which linked these to the literacy standards and curriculum? How could they satisfy the audit requirements and criticisms of the Further Education Funding Council that learners should progress when many of their steps forward were so small that they were not ready to move on to next levels of awards or accreditation? How could colleagues be convinced that the funding methodology would allow recognition of achievement of a learner's own objective? When would managers and policy-makers realise that the MIS records did not accurately indicate the true achievement of learners?

Did learners feel they were succeeding? Did they set themselves the same goals and measurements which the system recorded? What did they set out to achieve? Did they feel that they made progress? The National Foundation for Educational Research (NFER) report commissioned by the BSA was due; what would students say about their progress? Tutors often suggested that students did not want to follow an accredited programme; was this really reflecting the voice of the learners or was it because the associated paperwork was too burdensome? What did learners want to learn, what helped them to succeed and how did they know whether they were succeeding?

The research questions which framed the subsequent investigation arose from both practice and study; they were concerned with tutors' and learners' concepts of successful teaching and learning and with factors leading to that success.

Concepts of success

Understanding the concept of success in literacy education was of concern to Charnley and Jones in 1979 and has been studied more recently by others such as Du Vivier (1992), Abell (1992), Freebody and Welch (1993), Gardner (1995), MacKillop (1997) and Bynner *et al* (2001). They all suggested, amongst other things, that it was concerned with a growth in confidence and related to previous negative experiences of learning as well as poor health and sense of well-being. Changes in behaviour and relationships seemed to characterise the growth in confidence. The Office for National Statistics (1997) and the OECD study of 2000 agreed with these findings.

Others, such as Sticht (1990) and Moser (1999), argued that success should be measured against externally-set standards or by accreditation and qualifications set by external bodies. The proliferation of awards and certificates offered by the Royal Society of Arts (RSA, now OCR), City and Guilds, the Open College Network and the Associated Examining Board (AEB) indicated the preferences of many organisations, in order to meet the perceived demands of the FEFC funding methodology. Success for the FEFC appeared to be measured by the number of 'qualifications' gained; institutions were rewarded on that basis.

More researchers suggested that setting a personal goal and monitoring the movement towards its achievement, with the learner, indicated success. The focus on the learner, and the things s/he wanted to learn, were expounded by Metz (1990), Finlay and Harrison (1992), Rhoder and French (1994), Finlay (1997) and Street (1997).

The challenge is whether success is indicated by measurements based on external standards or a less easily measurable, more personal issue of achievement of individual targets and increases in confidence. It is possible that it is a combination of these apparently polarised positions.

Research methods

Having examined and assessed various research methods a case study approach was adopted using focused interviews, based upon one college of further education (Powney and Watts, 1987; Walker, 1995; Scott, 1996; Cohen and Manion, 1998; Stake, 1998; Hannon, 2000). Qualitative approaches complemented quantitative methods to gain insights from both (Silverman, 1993; Schratz and Walker, 1995; Scott, 1996). Recognition was given to the researcher's position as a manager of the staff and the former tutor of some of the students and the influence this might have upon the study. The necessity to be reflexive throughout the investigation was also recognised (Hammersley and Atkinson, 1983; Ozga and Gewirtz, 1994; Troyna, 1994; Woods, 1996).

The role was felt to be that of a practitioner or teacher researcher (Stenhouse, 1975; Schön, 1983; OECD, 1995; Skeggs, 1994; Bryant, 1996; Hamilton, 1998; Hannon, 2000). Using the basic skills centre in a further education college, members of the management were contacted to gain permission for the study to be carried out, as well as members of the teaching staff. Working together, tutors ascertained the most appropriate way to contact learners. Schedules were drafted to use in the informal interviews with both staff and students, and shared with tutors prior to the beginning of the process. A sample boundary for students was established of attendance of at least one term so that time for some learning development had been allowed.

Most of the interviews were taped and transcribed and the resulting text was examined for topics, themes and commonalities of response as well as anomalies and tensions, using "inductive analysis" (Janesick, 1998, p47). These were transferred to two large grids capturing what tutors and students said. An attempt was made to be as rigorous as possible in the analysis process while remaining faithful to the respondents.

Tutor interviews

The ten female tutors interviewed reflected the gender of tutors across the country but they were better qualified and taught more than many of their counterparts (Moser, 1999). They all taught in the college basic skills centre and reported that they delivered tuition on an individual basis, often describing the centre as a workshop. They managed groups of five to 12 learners, indicating that the context reflected that which is carried out elsewhere (Moser, 1999).

The interviews asked why students sought tuition and what they asked to learn. Questions were raised about what tutors aim to do, the teaching methods used and how they decide whether students are successful in their learning. They were asked to identify what seems to lead to success.

The resulting analysis revealed that between them, tutors identified 14 classifications of teaching approaches, with seven of them being mentioned by six or more respondents. In the order of frequency these were:

- base tuition on individual interests/ relevances;
- provide personal and social support for each student;
- use a variety of teaching styles;
- assess, plan and review (on-going cycle);
- use computer-assisted learning;
- use a range of spelling strategies;
- use real print.

Tutors' perceptions of success

In response to questions about how they knew whether students were being successful they suggested (in order of frequency):

- increases in confidence, motivation, assertiveness and feeling better about themselves;
- demonstrating learning through a review of goals or targets;
- using something which has been learned;
- receiving feedback from friends or family;
- doing something the student could not do before;
- attending regularly;
- indicating through assessment or tests;
- aspiring to do something else;
- taking responsibility for learning;
- finding out by asking the student;
- receiving computer feedback.

All tutors said that they used more than one indicator, with one tutor mentioning eight. All tutors spoke about increases in confidence; there was no other indicator to which they all made reference. They said such things as:

> "…it's about confidence; if they'll talk to people, if they feel that they're making progress…they'll take stuff home and talk amongst friends and they show it to people" (Tutor C).

> "…you know they must be making progress if they're taking pleasure in their work and are keen to continue. They'll talk to others about what they're doing…they seem brighter and happier" (Tutor J).

Tutor B explained:

> "I think they gain in confidence…they think, 'Yes, I can do this!' Then they do a bit more…I'll try this and do this…they're enjoying what they're doing…they're motivated…They say, 'I want to do this'…
>
> It's not accreditation. I don't think that matters to the majority, it's not high on the list. Some of them need it, otherwise they think they've not done anything about their difficulty. For the majority, it's for fulfilment. I think that some of them think

there's something wrong with them…someone in the past has told them – a teacher, a parent, a partner…a partner very often…they've been told, 'You'll never do anything' and so they're out to prove them wrong.

And they see they can, and they prove to themselves they can do it. A lot of it is confidence and self-esteem" (Tutor B).

Reviewing work was another frequently mentioned way in which tutors believed they knew whether students were learning successfully; it was referred to by eight of them. This is a process of learning rather than an outcome of it. Six of them indicated how students talk about using something they had learned in daily life. This included:

"…reading recipes and gas bills and other things that come in the post" (Tutor G).

"…using new skills and knowledge such as when shopping, letters, at work…they say they, 'Had a go'" (Tutor I).

"They read signs around town…they do something like read the paper and the adverts…they tell you" (Tutor J).

Five of the ten tutors spoke about how feedback from family and colleagues was an important indicator of success.

"…sometimes students will bring their parents or partners in…it shows what is important and what they are interested in…husbands and wives will come in and say how well they are doing. Sometimes they then come too" (Tutor C).

"…they use what they've learned at home, with their families. They tell me that they've done something at home and their families say, 'How do you know that?' (Tutor H).

"…some come on quite a lot, like G. whose work mates have helped him. He was quite laid back about it and told them at work. They had to admit he was doing well; they noticed it" (Tutor B).

What seems to lead to success?

In identifying what seems to lead to success three categories emerged:

- student-centred, individual programmes of learning;
- confidence in the relationship with the tutor;
- time, for students to attend and learn and for tutors to plan and prepare.

All tutors referred to the student-centred approach and the centrality of the individual learning plan. They said such things as:

> *"Having a plan, based on what they want…listen to them…watch them…be flexible…plug the gaps…review and write the plan again"* (Tutor B).

> *"You assess them and set targets with them. They seem to trust you when the targets are set and in the plan – they know what they're doing. You give them time to do it and then review with them"* (Tutor A).

Nine of the ten tutors felt that a good relationship with the tutor, volunteer and organisation was vital to success, saying,

> *"They have to be happy with the tutor. I think they have to be motivated by the tutor; I want to inspire them"* (Tutor B).

> *"They have confidence in the tutor; you have to be organised, keep your promises and be structured about what you're doing"* (Tutor E).

> *"They have to feel comfortable in the centre; they're not alone; they have to have confidence in the tutor and the college"* (Tutor I).

Student interviews

Thirty students were interviewed, for over an hour each; 19 were male and 11 female. (Their names have been changed to protect their anonymity.) They had studied between 72 and 450 hours in the previous year, with the majority (13) attending for 144 hours. Sixteen of them were unemployed, ten were in work, two of them described themselves as volunteers, one was a full-time carer and one retired.

The data gathered were classified into seven categories:

- why and how students felt about seeking tuition and what they wanted to learn;
- how they were taught and what activities they covered;
- whether they felt they were being successful and what indicators they used;
- what difference, if any, learning had made to them;
- what had helped them to learn;
- whether there were things at which they had not succeeded;
- what they might like to do next.

The students revealed general life-related goals as reasons for seeking tuition as well as educationally specific goals. More than three-quarters of the students spoke about how nervous they were about joining a group, with six people saying that they were comfortable with the idea. Of these six, three had come with a friend or relative. Anxieties were expressed in such ways as:

"Terrified!" (John).

"Very nervous" (David).

"I was very embarrassed; I still am" (Rick).

"I felt ashamed. When I saw all the computers I thought everyone would be clever… when I first came, I was ready to pack up because I thought if someone on the computer who I know, sees me doing this, well, I'd be right embarrassed. Well, I thought these were whiz kids, you know. I told her [the tutor] I wasn't going to come back. But she explained that this is basic and they all come to a class like me. I felt… oh, I don't know, ashamed really" (Paul)

In talking about how they are taught, each student spoke about several activities; the most frequently referred to were:

- individual work;
- using computers;
- writing;
- spelling;
- reading;
- technical skills (grammar, punctuation).

All of these were mentioned by approximately half of the students or more.

Students' perceptions of success

In asking students about whether they were being successful in their learning, the majority were adamant that they were and could present evidence to back up their claims. Only three of them suggested partial success, indicating that perhaps they had not achieved as much as they had hoped:

"I can read the paperwork, do the alphabet and spelling, especially on the computer, but writing and spelling on paper.... I have had some success but not got there yet" (Rick).

"I'm partly successful but I need to keep going" (Freda).

"I'm getting there but I still need some help" (Amanda).

The responses of all students were classified into literacy indicators and those which suggested differences in life. All students could identify literacy indicators such as reading the newspaper, talking to people in offices and shops, reading and writing and spelling more or better, pronunciation, using computers, tackling spelling, writing a name and address, writing stories and paragraphs, reading signs in the road, spotting mistakes, finding recipes, doing crosswords, using punctuation and using a dictionary. They appeared to compare their previous and current literacy behaviour, in order to assess their success.

In response to questions about what difference learning had made to them, students described changes in behaviour, which suggested that not only had they learned something but also that they were using the new knowledge or skill in life and work. These included such things as reading and purchasing newspapers and magazines, reading forms and letters, writing letters and cards at home, using reading and writing at work and speaking to people in official roles, 'in authority'. In addition, they spoke of increased confidence, doing new things, experiencing greater independence and comments from family or work colleagues. However, none of the indicators exceeded a response rate of one third of the cohort except that which related to increased confidence, which was reported by 28 (93%).

Table 1: The indicators of success which have made a difference – identified by students
F = Female M = Male

	Read newspaper magazines	Read forms and letters	Write at home eg letters, cards	Read, write at work	Use phone & speak to people in authority	At home read books and look things up	Read signs	Increased confidence feel better	Doing things outside home, increased independence	Work friend or family notice
F1				√				√		
F2		√			√			√	√	√
F3						√	√	√	√	√
F4	√				√			√		√
F5			√		√	√		√	√	√
F6								√		
F7						√		√		
F8	√							√	√	
F9				√	√			√		√
F10		√						√		
F11								√		
M1					√			√		
M2			√					√		
M3		√	√					√		
M4			√	√		√		√		√
M5	√		√					√		
M6			√		√			√		
M7			√					√	√	
M8					√					
M9				√			√	√		√
M10				√	√			√		
M11	√	√						√		√
M12								√		
M13	√		√					√		
M14				√				√		
M15				√				√		√
M16				√		√		√	√	
M17					√			√		
M18				√		√		√	√	
M19	√	√								
Total F	2 (18%)	2 (18%)	1 (9%)	2 (18%)	4 (36%)	3 (27%)	1 (9%)	11 (100%)	4 (36%)	5 (45%)
Total M	4 (21%)	3 (16%)	7 (37%)	7 (37%)	5 (26%)	3 (16%)	1 (5%)	17 (89%)	3 (16%)	4 (21%)
TOTAL	6 (20%)	5 (17%)	8 (27%)	9 (30%)	9 (30%)	6 (20%)	2 (7%)	28 (93%)	7 (23%)	9 (30%)

Percentages equal the proportion of the female, male and total cohorts.

What helped students to learn

The next table summarises what students believed led to success and helped them most. The overwhelming number of responses was associated with the skills of the tutor or volunteer tutor and the fact that tuition was not like school. The relationship with teaching staff appeared different from their previous educational experiences and 77% of students further stated that what they did in the centre was also different. They made such comments as:

"It's the tutors. You've got to get on. They help, if you tell them what's the matter, they find out how to help you" (Bob).

"What helps? The teachers; they don't present like teachers. They're just people who help. They don't put you down. At work there are people who try to put you down and you have to stand up to them; now I can. But here, it's not like that" (John).

"One thing that's made me change a lot of things, is a lady sat out there. She's a great help; she sat with me all the way through. We've got on like two partners. She's a volunteer, yes she's only just passed. Like she says, I'm helping her and she's helping me so we're both helping each other. I don't think I'd have done owt if it wasn't for her. I mean, we talk a lot together and we put it down like we've discussed. To be honest, it's worked out a treat. We've worked as a team" (Jo).

In relation to their teaching experiences they said:

"It's not like school. The tutors treat you like you're an adult. We have a big room, which helps you to talk to people and we have computers as well as access to the library. We use them when we want" (Tim).

"It's not like being in a classroom where, when you were at school, with 20 or so children and the teacher telling everybody. When I was at school they marked your book and gave it back to you and that was it. They never went through it with you. When I was at school they weren't particularly bothered anyway. They weren't bothered if you kept quiet" (Ewan).

"I was bullied at school. You don't get that here, you think for yourself and it's more ordered than there" (Carol).

"We never had teaching like this at school, it's personal, it's totally different from school" (David).

Table 2: What seemed to lead to success/help most (students)

	Male	Female	Total
1. The tutor/volunteer tutor	15 (79%)	10 (91%)	25 (83%)
2. There are different ways of doing things – not like school	12 (63%)	11 (100%)	23 (77%)
3. Computers	7 (37%)	3 (27%)	10 (33%)
4. Small groups and 1:1	4 (21%)	3 (27%)	7 (23%)
5. There is no pressure	6 (32%)	0 (0%)	6 (20%)
6. Other students	2 (11%)	3 (27%)	5 (17%)
7. It's fun/enjoyable	1 (5%)	2 (18%)	3 (10%)
8. Regular attendance	1 (5%)	2 (18%)	3 (10%)
9. Its what I am interested in	1 (5%)	2 (18%)	3 (10%)
10. A certificate	2 (11%)	0 (0%)	2 (7%)
11. Taping	1 (5%)	0 (0%)	1 (3%)

Percentages equal the proportion of the female, male and total cohorts

Journeys of confidence

John lost his job at nineteen years of age due to his inability to read and, in response to questions about the difference learning had made, said,

> *"What difference has it made? I've a much better job and I keep going on. I'll confront people now; I would never have done that. I've done exams at work, I've done presentations and given a talk for 15 minutes. I prepare OHTs. My whole life is different. I've been coming for a long time but I'm still making progress. I've pushed myself but it takes lots of courage. I train others now; I could never have imagined that. I've made huge leaps of progress. I feel more confident these last few years and I take that confidence with me"* (John).

During his attendance over a decade he had moved from being a supermarket shelf-filler to a trainer; the learning gains had been huge but he spoke clearly about his growth in confidence.

Carol had been in college for over two years and responded to a similar question about the difference it had made to her:

> *"I feel more pleased and happier in myself and more relaxed in myself; I think, 'Yes, I can do it'. And now, I feel I can ask for help as well because I used to think, 'Oh no, I think it's wrong….', cos I felt stupid. And now I can do my work better so it's give me more confidence. More confidence is coming out all the time"* (Carol).

She explained how her ability to tackle form filling was an indicator of increased confidence:

> *"I'll have a go if they're only small forms but if they're right big ones my husband does them. So we can help each other and he helps me, which has given me a lot more confidence, but I do try and have a go now on my own, whereas before I didn't. I was scared of getting them wrong. Well, I'm finding now that I've got a lot more confidence in myself whereas before I never did"* (Carol).

Unlike John, Carol had not made very great learning gains, if external measurements of literacy had been used, but she reported how her growth in confidence in tackling literacy activities made a difference to her sense of well-being and relationships.

Similarly, Rick indicated that he had not succeeded in the way he had hoped, in spite of attending for several years. He explained in an articulate way how he ran his own business which he described as very successful. He described how he could estimate and measure very accurately for his work as a fitter and joiner but couldn't write down orders and quotations. He said,

"I need to do this for my work. It's stopped me doing what I want – run my business. I cheat; I have a portfolio of all the options which people can choose and then my wife helps me by typing up what they want. I can't write it down in front of a client; I remember it, copy it in the car and take it home. I'm still embarrassed out there, but not in here, now. I'm more confident with my reading but writing and spelling...but I've not got there yet" (Rick).

Whilst Rick was confident and successful in his work, in literacy he felt frustrated; however, he suggested that some degree of success was indicated by a growth in confidence.

Sheila explained what a dramatic difference learning had made to her:

"I used to say, 'I forgot my glasses'. I could hardly speak to anybody and it's given me a lot more confidence in myself. I used to be frightened to go anywhere. Oh yes, cafes; I'm not frightened to go anywhere now; I can go and have a cup of coffee. Coming here, it's made a new lease of life for me. I think that I've got more confidence at doing things. I do my cooking and I like my gardening and I go to bingo on Wednesdays. That's another thing, I used to be frightened of marking wrong numbers.

My husband thinks it's marvellous. He said it's the best thing that's happened, you know, reading and other things.

I got this award and I stood on the stage, you know. I saw them faces and I thanked them all at college for what they'd done for me and I said the one thing that's come out of it is my reading Catherine Cookson. Everybody gave a cheer" (Sheila).

Sheila, who had been in literacy education for several years, had been referred by her doctor, following experiences of mental ill-health. She suggested that engagement in learning had made a significant contribution to her levels of confidence as well as literacy.

Sharon also suggested improvements in health and well-being after attending for several years:

"Oh, it has helped me a lot. I can sleep now whereas I couldn't before. I'm mixing with people and am more confident to talk and do my work. I feel happy since I've been coming here. When I was stuck at home I was right unhappy. I couldn't get to

sleep 'til three o'clock in the morning. Now, I've got something to look forward to"
(Sharon).

Whilst no formal assessment of literacy gains was made as part of the research,
there were suggestions that Sharon had made only tiny steps of progress

*"I do rhythm and rhyme, I go on computers; my reading's come on a bit but I've still
got to keep practising"* (Sharon).

All these students reported growth in confidence, regardless of whether they had
made marked progress in literacy. It seems that this outcome is of real significance
to a wide range of learners of literacy education.

When the literacy indicators of success, reported by both tutors and students, were
juxtaposed, differences and similarities were revealed.

Figure 1 shows how each group believed they knew whether success was being
achieved.

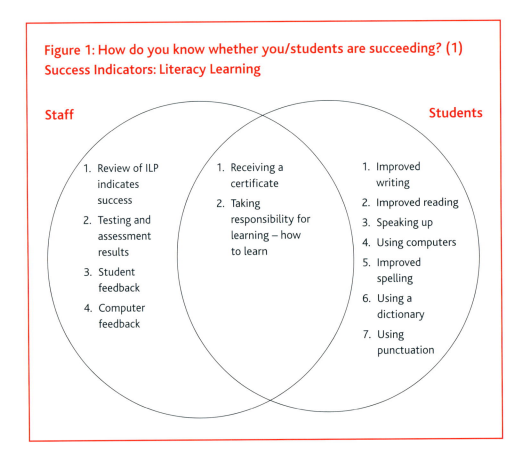

**Figure 1: How do you know whether you/students are succeeding? (1)
Success Indicators: Literacy Learning**

Staff

1. Review of ILP indicates success
2. Testing and assessment results
3. Student feedback
4. Computer feedback

1. Receiving a certificate
2. Taking responsibility for learning – how to learn

Students

1. Improved writing
2. Improved reading
3. Speaking up
4. Using computers
5. Improved spelling
6. Using a dictionary
7. Using punctuation

Figure 2 demonstrates what differences students and tutors felt that successful learning made. Increase in confidence was the most commonly reported difference, which indicated successful learning, from both tutors and students.

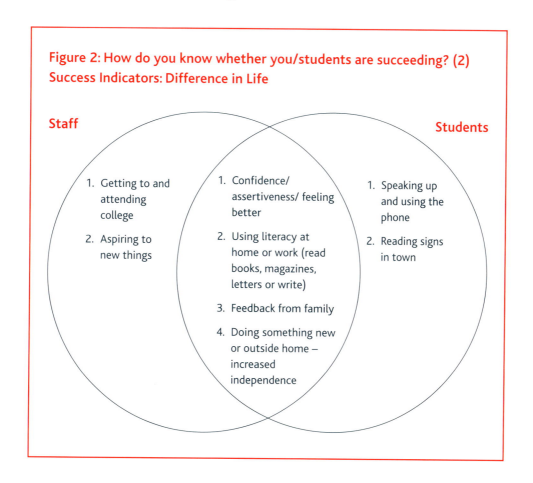

Figure 2: How do you know whether you/students are succeeding? (2) Success Indicators: Difference in Life

Staff

Students

1. Getting to and attending college
2. Aspiring to new things

1. Confidence/ assertiveness/ feeling better
2. Using literacy at home or work (read books, magazines, letters or write)
3. Feedback from family
4. Doing something new or outside home – increased independence

1. Speaking up and using the phone
2. Reading signs in town

Exploring confidence

This study revealed the importance of increases in confidence to tutors and students; further exploration of the concept seems justified. Many other studies have referred to this (Charnley and Jones, 1979; Du Vivier, 1992; Crowther and Tett, 1997; Mackillop, 1997; FEFC, 1999; Brooks *et al*, 2001) and this investigation could cast further illumination into what lies behind the concept, in relation to literacy education.

Both students and tutors suggested that changes in behaviour and students' feelings about themselves as learners, particularly increases in confidence, indicated to them that success was being achieved. Regardless of the level of study, or ability or the apparent amount of measurable literacy progress, raised confidence was an indicator of success. The external, observable signs of increased involvement, on a day-to-day basis, seemed to suggest to not only students and tutors but also families and employers that learners were more confident in these areas of their lives. There was a high level of agreement about how both students and tutors know that successful learning is taking place.

Students reported many activities in their lives which demanded high levels of confidence. Ewan described how his job demanded talking to the public; Rick and Sara spoke about running their own business; Matt had spent a lifetime travelling around Europe; and John told of promotion at work. They all reported increases in confidence in relation to literacy, suggesting that they did not lack general confidence, but a form of 'situated confidence'. Mace reported similar experiences,

"If someone in that room said that she had gained in confidence since she began meeting her tutor six months before, that statement has to be recognised for what it is; a statement made in a specific context. We often were not aware, and forgot to think about or imagine the other settings in which that same person may already be confident, far more confident than we..." (Mace 1992, p10).

It is possible to argue that confidence is a catch-all word, which captures a number of feelings, fuelled by changed actions and behaviours in relation to literacy learning which cannot be easily captured using different vocabulary. Any gains, no matter how small, in literacy skill, knowledge, understanding or application appear to contribute to confidence. An emerging question is associated with what students, tutors, providers and policy-makers want to happen as a result of successful literacy education. The response is likely to be greater involvement in literacy activities in daily living and working. The outcome of raised confidence, regardless of the externally measurable progress, was also greater engagement in literacy activities; the results seem to be similar.

Not only is confidence an indicator of success, it is also an outcome of participation. If it is as important as this study suggests, it seems equally important that it is identified as an objective of teaching. It can then be formatively reviewed, assessed and acknowledged in the learning process by students and tutors as well as those who provide the service and fund it. In studying soft outcomes, Dewson *et al* (2000) found that few projects were able to measure soft outcomes. Brooks *et al* (2000) and Machin *et al* (2001) revealed that there is little evidence of a correlation between growth in confidence and progress in literacy. This appears to endorse the importance of trying to capture growth in confidence in the learning process. Brooks *et al* (2001) identified that not all learners make significant progress in literacy education. It seems that almost all learners make gains in confidence which impact on their engagement with and application of literacy in daily living.

The experiences of fear, vulnerability and insecurity in relation to literacy education were clearly articulated by students and tutors. They indicated what they believed helped them to learn, identifying such things as the relationship with the tutor and the learning environment and methods. The individual approaches helped to create a sense of trust and the social security necessary to dispel fear and anxiety. One of the secrets of confidence-building, according to Covington (1992), is the need to avoid repeating earlier failures; the experiences of students suggest that this was facilitated for them. The raised sense of 'feeling good' about themselves could lead to increased involvement in areas of life, hitherto felt to be inaccessible. The virtuous spiral of increased confidence, leading to increased literacy involvement and further confidence, seems evident.

The concept of success as a qualitative indicator of confidence (Charnley and Jones, 1979) or measured against prescribed standards (Moser, 1999) are not necessarily polarised but could be seen as complementary. More than three-quarters of students reported improvements in writing and two-thirds reported improved reading. This indicates that they believed they were learning in the areas that had motivated them in the first place. The improvements were self-assessed. These measurements are not necessarily those used by tutors to demonstrate whether students have developed competency or have achieved standards at a particular level. The significance is that both gains in confidence and progress in literacy appear to have been made.

It is possible to surmise from this study that tutors in literacy education realise the importance of confidence as an indicator of successful teaching and learning but do not record its development because it is difficult to measure and record. However, one can conclude that if it is so significant to both learners and tutors, as an indication that they are being successful in their endeavours, attempts *should* be made to measure and record it. The use of life indicators, related to literacy application in daily living and working, was believed to be evidence of successful learning. It is unlikely that these indicators are recorded except in conversation or through observation and verbal feedback, as anecdotal evidence. It can be concluded that these indicators must be ultimate goals of literacy education and therefore should be used as evidence of success. Things that are planned, taught, reviewed and assessed are recorded on the individual learning plan. These could be described as literacy indicators; assessment of them is generally by others as well as the learner. Indicators that are unplanned, observed, reflected upon (by self or tutor) or fed back could be described as being internally assessed and seem strongly related to confidence, feelings, self-esteem and well-being. The imbalance appears to be between things which are easily measured and things which are difficult to define, measure and evidence (Mace, 1992).

Implications for further research

In the light of the centrality of confidence as an indicator of successful teaching and learning in adult literacy education, future research should be conducted in order to understand the concept and to evidence its growth and development. Ignoring its importance is likely to result in perpetuating a situation where we only measure those things which it is easy to measure. Things which are seen as important outcomes for students and tutors may not be acknowledged or celebrated.

Asking questions about whether students drop out of learning because confidence had not been nurtured would also help in developing effective literacy educational practices.

Learners and tutors reported that changes in behaviour outside the learning situation were indicative of successful learning. They also reported that students increasingly engaged in literacy practices at home and work. We should also investigate whether initial and formative assessment practices could be developed to capture such evidence of success.

As the relationship between tutors and students seems to lead to successful learning, reflection on the training and development of tutors of adult literacy should include ways of forming constructive relationships which support learning and encourage autonomy.

We should ask questions about whether current policies are gaining the results they are designed to achieve. Evaluation studies of the impact of current strategies would help give insight into effectiveness.

Listening to tutors and students revealed insights which previously had been predominantly anecdotal evidence of successful teaching and learning. Engaging practitioners as researchers must be encouraged in order to draw on their valuable experiences and insights.

Similarly, listening to learners' experiences of literacy education could contribute significant insights into the development of practice and policy. Those who have intimate understanding of the daily struggles to engage in complex literacy processes should be supported so that their voices are heard and responded to.

In addition to conducting investigations into different ways of recording achievement, practitioners should be involved in considering how they assess learning, both formatively and summatively. If much of the evidence of success is revealed outside the learning situation, practitioners should include feedback from learners about their literacy practices at home and work.

Implications for working with and training volunteers in adult literacy education also arise from this study. The importance of volunteers was indicated by both tutors and students; and the relationship between them was believed to be a key to success. Clarity about roles and relationships as well as vital skills should be developed by practitioners who have responsibility for such work.

Conclusion

This study suggests that success in literacy learning is not necessarily evidenced by achieving standards set by external bodies but by goals which tutors and students discuss and agree. Whilst they all communicated the importance of working at things which form the national Adult Literacy Core Curriculum, a significant number of students appeared unable to achieve the standards suggested, even after several years' study. However, they did report increases in confidence. Other students had made huge progress but also reported that confidence was an important indication that they were learning successfully.

Growth in confidence is a key outcome of successful literacy education and it should be recognised, assessed, recorded and celebrated in the process of teaching and learning.

Bibliography

Abell, S. (1992). *Effective Approaches in Adult Literacy,* London, Adult Literacy and Basic Skills Unit

Adult Literacy and Basic Skills Unit (1993). *A Survey of Users of ESOL Programmes in England and Wales*, London, ALBSU

Adult Literacy and Basic Skills Unit (1994). *Planning the Programmes, Basic Skills in Further Education*, London, ALBSU

Adult Literacy Unit (1978). *Newsletter No. 2*, London, Adult Literacy Unit

Avis, J. (1996). *The Myth of the Post-Fordist Society, in Knowledge and Nationhood, Education, Politics and Work*, Cassell Education

Barton, D., Hamilton, M. and Ivanič, R. (2000). *Situated Literacies: Reading and Writing in Context*, London, Routledge

Basic Skills Agency (1998). *Notes from the briefing meeting*, 1/10/98

Basic Skills Agency (2001). *Adult Literacy Core Curriculum*, London, BSA

Brooks, G. *et al* (2000). *Assembling the Fragments: A review of research on Adult Basic Skills*. Norwich, DfEE

Brooks, G. *et al* (2001). *Progress in Adult Literacy. Do Learners Learn?* London, Basic Skills Agency

Bryant, I. (1996). *Action research and reflective practice in Understanding Educational Research*, Scott, D. and Usher, R. (Eds.) London, Routledge

Bynner, J. *et al* (2001). *Improving Adult Basic Skills, Benefits to the Individual and to Society*, Norwich, DfEE

Charnley, A.H. and Jones, H.A. (1979). *The Concept of Success in Adult Literacy*, London, ALBSU

Charnley, A.H. and Withnall, A. (1989). *Developments in Basic Education, Special Development Projects 1978–85*, London, ALBSU

Cohen, L. and Manion, L. (1998). *Research Methods in Education*, London, Routledge

Covington, M. (1992). *Making the Grade: A self-worth perspective on motivation and school reform*, Cambridge, Cambridge University Press

Crowther, J. and Tett, L. (1997). Literacies not Literacy, in *Adults Learning*, vol 8, no 8, April, Leicester, NIACE

DfEE (1998). *The Learning Age: a renaissance for a new Britain*, The Stationery Office, DfEE

DfEE (2001). *Improving Adult Basic Skills: Benefits to the individual and to society*, Nottingham, DfEE

DfEE (2001). *Skills for life: the national strategy for improving adult literacy and numeracy skills*, Nottingham, DfEE

Dewsons, S., Eccles, J., Tackey, N. and Jackson, A. (2000). *Measuring Soft Outcomes and Distance Travelled: A review of current practice*, Sheffield, DfEE

Du Vivier, E. (1992). *Learning to be literate. A study of Students' Perceptions of the Goals and Outcomes of Adult Literacy Tuition*, Dublin, Dublin Literacy Scheme

Fingeret, H. and Drennon, C. (1997). *Literacy for Life, New York*, Teachers' College Press

Finlay, A. (1997). *Informal Measures Challenge the Suitability of the Basic Skills Agency's Reading Test*, in Reading, p29

Finlay, A. and Harrison, C. (1992). Measuring success in reading in Adult Basic Education: A UK perspective, in *Adult Literacy: A Compendium of Articles from the Journal of Reading*, Delaware, USA, International Reading Association

Freebody, P. and Welch, A. (Eds.)(1993). *Knowledge, Culture and Power: International Perspectives on Literacy as Policy and Practice*, London, Falmer Press

Further Education Funding Council (1999). *Basic Education, Making a Difference*, Coventry, FEFC

Gardner, C. (1995). A critical transformative approach to social reality, in, *Practice in Reading Values, Reflection on Adult Literacy Teaching*, Australia, National Language and Literacy Institute

Hamilton, D. (1998). *The Silence of the Shadows: Educational Research and the ESRC in Challenges for Educational Research*, Rudduck, J. and McIntyre, D. (Eds.) London, Paul Chapman Publishing

Hamilton, M. (1996). Literacy and Adult Basic Education, in *A History of Modern British Adult Education*, Fieldhouse,R. and Associates (Eds.) Leicester, NIACE

Hammersley, M. and Atkinson, P. (1983). *Ethnographic Principles in Practice*, London, Tavistock

Hannon, P. (2000). *Reflecting on Literacy in Education*, London, Routledge Falmer

Hourigan, M. (1994). *Literacy as Social Exchange: Intersections of class, gender and culture,* Albany USA, State University of New York Press

Janesick, V. (1998). *The Dance of Qualitative Research Design in Strategies of Qualitative Inquiry*, Denzin, N. and Lincoln,Y. (Eds) London, Sage

Mace, J. (1992). *Talking about Literacy: Principles and Practice of Adult Literacy Education*, London, Routledge

MacKillop, J. (1997). *Assessment in Adult Literacy Programs in the United States*, unpublished PhD thesis, University of Sheffield

Moser, C. (1999). *A Fresh Start: Improving Literacy and Numeracy, Report of the working group*, chaired by Sir Claus Moser, Sudbury, DfEE

OECD (1995). *Educational Research and Development, Trends, Issues and Challenges*, Paris, OECD

Office for National Statistics (ONS) (1997). *Adult Literacy in Britain*, London, The Stationery Office

Ozga, J. and Gewirtz, S. (1994). *Sex, Lies and Audiotape: Interviewing the Education Policy Elite in Researching Education Policy: Ethical and Methodological Issues*, Halpin, D. and Troyna, B. (Eds.) London, Falmer Press

Powney, J. and Watts, M. (1987). *Interviewing in Educational Research*, London, Routledge and Kegan Paul

Qualifications and Curriculum Authority (QCA) (2000). *Standards for adult literacy*, Sudbury, QCA

Rhoder, C. and French, J. (1994). Workplace Literacy: From survival to empowerment and human development, *Journal of Reading*, 38:2, p110

Schön, D. (1983). *The Reflective Practitioner*, London, Temple Smith

Schratz, M. and Walker, R. (1995). *Research as Social Change: New Opportunities for qualitative research*, London, Routledge

Scott, D. (1996). *Methods and Data in Educational Research in Understanding Educational Research*, Scott, D. and Usher, R. (Eds.) London, Routledge

Silverman, D. (1993). *Interpreting Qualitative Data: Methods for Analysing Talk, Text and Interaction*, London, Sage

Skeggs, B. (1994). *The Constraints of Neutrality: The 1988 Education Reform Act and Feminist Research in Researching Education Policy: Ethical and Methodological Issues*, Halpin, D. and Troyna, B. (Eds.) London, Falmer Press

Social Exclusion Unit (2001). *A New Commitment to Neighbourhood Renewal*, London, Social Exclusion Unit

Stake, R. (1998). *Case Studies in Strategies of Qualitative Inquiry*, Denzin, N. and Lincoln,Y. (Eds.) London, Sage

Stenhouse, L. (1975). *An Introduction to Curriculum Research and Development*, London, Heinemann

Sticht, T. (1990). Measuring adult literacy: a response, in *Towards defining literacy*, Newark, DE, International Reading Association

Street, B. (1997). *Adult Literacy in the United Kingdom: A History of Research and Practice,* Lancaster, Research and Practice in Adult Literacy (RAPAL)

Thompson, J. (2001). *Rerooting Lifelong Learning, resourcing neighbourhood renewal*, Leicester, NIACE

Troyna, B. (1994). *Reforms, Research and Being Reflexive About Being Reflective in Researching Education Policy: Ethical and Methodological Issues*, Halpin, D. and Troyna, B. (Eds.) London, Falmer Press

Woods, P. (1996). *Researching the Art of Teaching*, London, Routledge